DEAR ALL,

Also by Maggie Anderson

Years That Answer
Cold Comfort
A Space Filled with Moving
Windfall: New and Selected Poems

Chapbooks:

The Great Horned Owl
Greatest Hits 1984-2004

DEAR ALL,

Maggie Anderson

Four Way Books
Tribeca

Please direct all inquiries to:
Editorial Office
Four Way Books
POB 535, Village Station
New York, NY 10014
www.fourwaybooks.com

Library of Congress Cataloging-in-Publication Data

Names: Anderson, Maggie, author.
Title: Dear all / Maggie Anderson.
Description: New York, NY : Four Way Books, [2017]
Identifiers: LCCN 2017000674 | ISBN 9781935536970 (pbk. : alk. paper)
Classification: LCC PS3551.N3745 A6 2017 | DDC 811/.54--dc23
LC record available at https://lccn.loc.gov/2017000674

2nd printing, 2017
This book is manufactured in the United States of America and printed on acid-free paper.

Four Way Books is a not-for-profit literary press. We are grateful for the assistance
we receive from individual donors, public arts agencies, and private foundations.

This publication is made possible with public funds from the National Endowment for the Arts

and from the New York State Council on the Arts, a state agency.

We are a proud member of the Community of Literary Magazines and Presses.

Distributed by University Press of New England
One Court Street, Lebanon, NH 03766

Til Anna,
din for evigt

CONTENTS

I.

Dear All, 3
Biography 5
Ordinary Morning 7
At Fifty 9
A Few Small Gestures of Concern 10
The Greeks of 1983 12
Black Overcoat 14
Ars Poetica 15
Fear of Farms 16
The House of Drink 18
My Father and Ezra Pound 20

II.

The Sleep Writer 25
Narrator with Stranger 26
The Wave 27
The Border 28
Ninth View of the North Sea 30
First Color Photographs of the War 31
Beautiful War 32
At the Blue Table 35
Note from My Father 37
Asleep still, I rise 38
Cleaning the Guns 40
Reading Yusef 42
A Drone Poem, Notes For 44

III.

Our Journey   51
Island   53
Waiting for Jane Austen in Walnut Creek, Ohio, at the end of the
    twentieth century   55
How the Brain Works   57
The Map   58
In the Rubble of the World   59
Signs Following   61
Too Much, Too Soon Migraine   62
In Real Life   64
The Thing You Can't Forget   66
A Blessing   67
In the Sidney Lanier Best Western Motel in Gainesville, Georgia,
    I think of the great Polish poet   68
And then I arrive at the powerful green hill   71

Notes

I

"Home-made, home-made! But aren't we all?"

—Elizabeth Bishop

Dear All,

You whose memory comes to me winter afternoons as the soon gone sun
       falls low and thin

You whom I knew long and well

You I knew but slightly, knew not well but cared to,
       had there been place enough and time

You who have come to hate me now

You who are the trees out the window to me, the shallow-rooted I have
       always loved

I greet you in my unsent letters, in both my random and my steady thoughts

You whom I failed to thank and you I failed to turn to

You I have tried and tried to speak with and have not been able to cross
       those seas

You I fought with in the snow in unsatisfactory shoes, marching up and down,
       shouting at each other, so hot we were, so cold, the drifts deepening

You I let down and you I picked up by the highway

You who have made a name for yourself

You who were called away and never came back,
        you who would not leave

You I worked with as we had never worked before, side by side
        in the studio with five windows glazed by yellow light

You I no longer know but fear dead—
        drugs, car wrecks, the several wars,
        the usual deaths of my generation—

And you who have gone the distance, beyond your disappointments,
        your cancers and their dire cures, my friends

I send you this letter, from the landscape of our years together

You must not wonder if I think of you still—
        I have remained steadfast here
        I have remembered you wholly into this day

Biography

Born, I was born.

    In sweat and tears I lay on a flowered blanket
before a chrome bucket of ice and a bladed fan.

    My mind is clear as polished glass,
my hair a tangle of black moss. I fall down

      on the grass in my harness, laughing.
Father is doing his skits and antics,

      running and sliding, dropping his trousers.
His starched shirts are strict and ghostly,

      they hang on a line over the bathtub.
Dying, Mother is dying, pale in her housecoat.
I am learning to run faster and faster,

      I can feel the blood in my ears.
Great Aunt Nell is large as a boat with her

      slick jersey dresses and embroidered handkerchiefs.
Flying, dust motes are flying, in a caduceus of light

      between the studio couch and the radiator.
Family arrives on the train in the rain

      carrying leather grips and hatboxes.
The self blooms,

      a chrysalis of sorrow.
Patricia, the soft reticule of her mouth

      pulls me from my dry cave.
I drink Father's gin with Robert,

      suck sweet smoke from a plug of blond hash.

The police are shoving into the crowd with tear gas and rifles,
        we do a day in a cell with no window.
I eat rice from a red lacquer bowl,
        green tea singes my tongue.
The riderless horse leads the procession.
        Fever carries me out of my body.
Father: "Listen at this;
        I have written it down."
Mother: "This is the table they have laid before me.
        I am not afraid."

Ordinary Morning

No more flags and banners!
No more of my endless good ideas!

In the hall of acquisitions the goods are readied.
In the walled rooms of learning the papers
are exchanged, the talk goes on
among drawn faces of young students.

In an ordinary February, what could happen?
I can imagine hunger, quavery
emptiness of nothing to eat and not knowing when.
Cut off, amputated in a cold basement with no news,
sharp static, a green transistor radio.

O mother and father I prematurely grieved,
where are you now that I need to lose you?
Ordinary mornings we rose and ate together,
dressed and went out into the world.

Phantom mother, your face a red and purple scrape,
your hat askew and your left ear bleeding,
in the back seat of a stranger's car. This thing
had happened: they found you sitting
on a stone wall where you had rolled away
from the car's tires, brought you
first to me and I did not know you.

In a glare of hospital lights, they took
my blood and gave it to you. What can happen
had happened, and our lives went limp and small.
How can I speak about this?
A flat sky, gray yet almost stunning
against heavy snow and a red sun rising.
I feel a cold that will
not stop, sound that has overrun
all meaning. Already the fires are close,
and the fields are burning.

At Fifty

My mother died at fifty of
a beautiful word, *leukemia*.
Nine years earlier
in autumn, she gave birth to me
when the maples in the park
began to turn as they do now.
I don't know how to walk here,
in the shifting space no meanings fill.
I have now outlived her.
I enter this foreshortened field,
wildly unmothered still.

A Few Small Gestures of Concern

Just north of Hartville, Ohio, where I drove today,
thick woods opened out to fields and cattle pastured
down to the lake. My mind was full of lists
of meetings, picking up medication and dry cleaning,
when suddenly for no reason, I was remembering
the time Lynn bought my lunch when
I had money enough to pay for my own, but because
she didn't know what to say to my grief,
she said *I want to buy your lunch,*
and it was expensive and good and I was grateful,
which made me think of Sandra whom I haven't seen in years,
walking beside the Willamette in Portland
in the cold sleet of a November night.
Nothing *happened.* We walked two city blocks
talking pleasantly about nothing in particular,
then she asked me if I wanted to borrow her gloves.
One afternoon, thirty years ago or more,
in my makeshift office in the Cathedral of Learning
with no furniture but a view of the Heinz Chapel spire
dark with rain and city grime, Ed stuck his head in the door
and said *It's a little alienating, isn't it?*
I wasn't sure if he meant Pittsburgh, or teaching,
the view, or life in general, but they all were,
and who would have thought I would remember
this so clearly for all these years?

In December 1971 I was visiting Jane Bennett in
California, Pennsylvania, where I called my father
from a wooden phone booth in a drugstore.
He was three days away from his death,
alone in his apartment, aphasic from the strokes.
I told him *I love you*, and he said
You're right. Those were his last words to me.
Sometimes when the years come close like this
everything that happened once seems to have been
happening forever: someone is putting cold cloths on my head
because it hurts, someone is sitting on the edge
of my bed where I am a fevered child in another world
far beyond hearing. Today I was only busy,
but when Anna touched my shoulder and told me
Take a little nap, you're exhausted, I could see I was,
so I lay down heavily, like the bales of hay
the good farmer of Hartville pitched out for his stock,
because the ground is frozen solid,
because the weeds are iced with hoarfrost.
And like the cattle, I ambled over the cold field
to take whatever might be offered now
from the flat bed of the mostly reliable wagon.

The Greeks of 1983

Ithaka gave you the marvelous journey.
Without her you wouldn't have set out.
> —C. P. Cavafy

Like one of Cavafy's young boys lurking
in the dark cafes of Alexandria for love,
I was close to the grammarians and the aristocrats,
living in Pennsylvania among the exiled
Greeks, who fed me ripe pistachios
and bites of lamb. They sang me songs
about the blue fields of garlic,
stone streets and white houses,
dark curtains drawn against the noon.
We drank strong coffee and they read my future
in the muddy grounds: *You will work*
along the edges all your life, never at the center
and never rich, but a good friend to the rich
especially in your later years.
I felt myself beloved of all the poets I read:
one of Auden's men, one of Sappho's women,
one of the animals of Gerald Stern.
My Greeks taught me the sound of waves
over black beaches, showed me seashells smaller
than a fingernail, the yellow moon—
fengare—reflected in the sea.
I learned six words for love

and the word for daisy which is my name—
how to say *the big sea, little orange tree,*
and *my child.* Sometimes they called me that—
to pethi mou—and in those days we were as
little children, making our first visions
setting out on our marvelous journeys.

Black Overcoat

From deep inside your black overcoat
        words, like a lost bird,
                are trying to find a way out—
now that you have begun
            you won't stop and I am waiting.
                  What is it? What happened?

A long time ago people were hurt and you caused it.
        I think you said you were *Sorry*
           or *Stupid*   or *Worried.*
You were not looking at me—
        but staring straight ahead
           through the windshield of the car
                at the night and the snow.

Trapped in a house, a bird will dive and circle back
        from room to room   from window to chair
             any steady edge
                between lifting up and landing—
    flight is what comes before telling
            or just after.

Ars Poetica

If it's a poem
You want,
Take a knife. . .
          —Charles Simic

When my mind was sliced open
and I could not read or write,
I carried knives to the whetstone
and honed them: paring knife
removes the skin, bares raw fruit
to air and light. Bowie knife guts
a deer carcass, penknife sharpens pencil lead.
Switchblade snaps out from the boot toe
guides a high kick to the throat.
Butter knives smear soft fat.
For meat, the cleaver splits tendon
and shank, scrapes blood from the bone.
I tested the heft of each one in my palm,
tried their blades against the air.
Then I tore dark hunks of bread,
pulled them apart with my bare hands.

Fear of Farms

After misreading the title of Muriel Rukeyser's Third Elegy, "The Fear of Form"

What would that be? The row upon row upon row
        then stupid turn of the tractor & back
grain elevator, combine, machine loose on
        the hillside, turned over, the bloody arm
the stink of hogs, of pigs, of money

Hot humid afternoons with hay sticking to hands
        & legs, hair matted to brow & neck
bees roused by the baler, swarming—
        a gray cloud of hot sting on face & arms
           white scar tissue where
the pot of boiling water for sterilizing Mason jars
        tilts & scalds forearm & top of foot
           in the shape of a sandal strap

Copperheads come quick from the cool foundation
        of the root cellar   first warm day
& nests of black snakes open out across the field
        adrenaline rush of hop & jump over them

Rat poison   rust & splinters, the catch of blades
        bats swooping low   the rabid, unpredictable
        rumble of black bears over the picnic table
        the girlish scream of the bobcat

Always something doesn't work needs to be fixed
        have to drive three places for parts
        all day on edge lost time in repair
        lost days of rain

Dark in the morning   already tired   up at first light
no mind   for reading or thinking, low ceilings
        picture a bumper crop   good corn, early
           more help with the haying
then supper & evening chores   an hour on the front porch
          check next day's weather on TV

Even in sleep   the fields are flooded
        cattle   loud & thin at the barn door
        the slightest lack of attention
can kill   self or other   constant alertness
        & no one to take my place

Who else would plough this land?
Who, if not I, will do all this?

The House of Drink

Early morning sun   green fields
mint green Chevrolet I drove through the hills
down   to the brown house beside the river
          the little house of drink
where mice built colonies in the walls and scratched
in and out at will   across the carpet and the bed
          where we drank and slept and loved.
Bats clung to the curtains   snakes rose from the well
          a pox of small unpleasant
creatures   a shed piled high with empty bottles
          that caught the sun through the slats
          green and brown, prismatic.

It was there the barn collapsed
          (my friend heard it too).
Up late drinking, smoking, laughing
we ran outside and watched
          the smoky dust rise up
          from a pile of boards and nails and shingles.
The whole gray thing fell down, as if we had breathed on it.

If I breathe too hard   I have to remember
          the hairpin curve where, drunk
I swerved and speeded up, drove through a fence
          into a pond where one of me died

while another of me hauled out the window
   on strong arms, my lithe young body
flipped and slid down
   the trunk   into pond muck and weeds.
I freed myself   and walked the three miles home
   scratched up, sore and stoned,
fell face down at my lover's feet
   from another world
bleeding on the kitchen floor.

My Father and Ezra Pound

I drank iced tea with whiskey in it,
      smoked Salems and read small poetry books
      on the cement slab we called a back porch,
wedged into a chair made from a broken barrel
      and painted bright orange.

Pound had just died
      and also my father.
I could trail a silly thought for hours;
for example, when I first read Pound he was alive,
        silent in Saint Elizabeths
and then I read him dead.
      Did this make any difference?
And what about Dad?
The year before he died
      he wrote fifty poems and six plays,
collaborating with his lover,
      the college business manager,
who had AIDS, though we didn't know it then.

My glass of tea was dark and didn't show the liquor
      but my breath did when she kissed me.
I was writing my early poems
      of vegetables and grief, reading the *Four Quartets*

and Algernon Swinburne for my exams,
mixing martinis in a chrome shaker
                              from my father's house.

All those years it took him to work out
          whom he loved, and he waited
                    until the end to break his silence—
envelopes of blue mimeographed pages—his legacy.
Once a week, my uncle called to see how I was doing.
My father was his only brother, so
          Pretty good, I always said.

I listened to The Doors and Joplin.
This was the seventies.
I was 23 years old, turning
          the thin pages of *The Cantos*.
No one came to visit.
          We had two dogs.
          We needed nothing then except each other,
                    and that we needed all the time.

II

"The world in its dark grace.
I have tried to record it."

—Charles Wright

The Sleep Writer

Lovely afternoon. The firing squad.
Bottles lined up in the sun.
Dahlias. Men in uniform. Daffodils.
Children with satchels coming home from school.
I am writing in my sleep. The journey here
was not very long, only a little cold,
the fast horses of exhaustion pulled me.
Too many people, I write, *are watching*
what we do. Too much sun on the green glass.
The firing squad. The lovely afternoon.

Narrator with Stranger

I am trying to write a story. Every day I assume
my usual posture, pen in hand poised
above paper. I shift the clumps of words,
first one way, then another, certain there
are more words, far from me.

I see now that this is a difficult narrative,
hot with dilemmas and sores.
When I try to continue, the air feels windless,
preternaturally still. Lambent smoke drifts
through leaves and coats the pine needles.

What if a stranger appears outside my door?
Say I drop what I am doing and rush out to greet her.
Say she does something unlikely—offers me
a box of ashes. I follow her out into the cold
then lose her under low-hanging limbs,

as I grow steadily absorbed in the way
shadows list against the toppled trees.
I spot the track of a wound in a drift of snow.
I decide to pick up the trail.

The Wave

I have studied the science of goodbyes.
          —Osip Mandelstam

This photograph is blurred but I recognize
the watery fields north of Amsterdam,
a windbreak of Lombardy poplars in the distance.
The camera stalls the scene, unbeautiful in milky light.
Only the caption—*Dutch Jews Departing for Auschwitz*—
lets us know the train is pulling away. The verb
is wrong—*departing* suggests volition.
Why are the people in the cars leaning
out the opened windows and waving
to maybe forty others who are crowded in a ditch
below the tracks, lifting their arms to wave back?
I have no idea who took this dim, benighted picture,
a smeared document that hangs in the exhibit hall
as evidence of the Final Solution. 1944, four years
before I am going to be born. The last train
is departing from Westerbork *nach* Auschwitz.
Jews are waving goodbye.

The Border

What's beyond the path
with the mounds of sticks and twigs,
the throaty pine cones and the slippery needles?
It's the gray scaly wall of the house
with the blue shutters
on Rue de la Dysse in Montpeyroux.
No, not that, but the dark forest
we almost could not make out,
beyond the ovens at the camp we
found by trailing small, vine-covered
wooden signs along the highway:
Gedenkstätte.
Sometimes before the headaches start,
I see things. Often it's a pale yellow light
between branches of black trees. There must
be wind, because the branches are moving.
It must be dusk, because the light is fading;
winter, because there are no leaves.
There is no sound but a thick humming
of something about to happen.
Just before the knife enters the nerve
above my left eye, I see the new refugees
running in their white headscarves
near the border. They are silent,

loaded down with bags and looking both ways
pulling the children behind them
as they haul themselves
up the steep hill toward the paved road.

Ninth View of the North Sea

What the ocean holds today is
leftover storm   old sea. Against the symmetry
of half-timbered houses stands the chaos

of the harbor dense with boats, the finery
of their flags, their ropes and riggings
dimmed by fog. The rescue boat is on alert,

its red and white semaphore a scald
against the wind. Nothing to fear.
I have come here to stare at the bruises.

I organize my days around the view:
the city buildings in sharp relief,
to the east, the neck of the estuary

where ferries carry cars
and bicycles across. And the rest?
Lost in translation: a snag

in certainty, a lonely rope of doubt,
father boots and mother tongue,
the small hand of a child at my throat.

First Color Photographs of the War

This Reuters photograph of women
in black chadors ballooning behind them in red air,
"carrying nonpotable water" through a bright orange
and yellow sandstorm is Mark Rothko's
Ochre and Red on Red, 1954, 93 by 64 inches.
In the lower right corner, a faint shadow of tank or donkey.
Matthew Brady stood behind a tripod at Gettysburg
trying to take his slow plates while the light was good.
Black and white—trees, fog, the faces of the wounded
in camp, the dead wrapped in blankets. In Basra
everything is moving and it seems nothing hurts,
bleed of sky around the mosques and statuary.
Some of these photographs are rich as Persian textiles,
others like backlit Dutch interiors with sinks and tables.
I would call it art, if there were more danger in it.

Beautiful War

painted, cropped, rearranged into
     dreamed landscape red on red
so that it does not look like war—
   no detonations,
        conflagrations
only the white onion tops of minarets,
       billowing black clothes
on the screen digitalized unsigned

How photogenic the desert is!
The black and whites, uncaptioned,
   could be Ansel Adams
      moon over desert
   quiet clean lucky
I cut out the pictures from the *New York Times*
   to make a diary of what happens.

March 2003 in Paris a blue peace sign hanging
from the fourth floor apartment window
   in the Ninth Arrondissement,
hundreds lining up outside Sacré-Cœur
   five o'clock Mass   a Tuesday
nuns in black habits praying for peace

I hurried back to my small hotel
                    between *Pigalle* and *Saint Georges*
to the news in French   on the tiny black and white TV
        bolted to the ceiling above the bed
where in *shock and awe* the new war started
                              the first clippings I saved from *Le Monde*—
        the *Herald Tribune* sold out at the kiosk—
the metro stations closed because of the demonstrations
a steady rain all day

Back home, in April I cut and pasted, full-page, full-color
photo of Jessica Lynch, first rescued soldier
        a girl from my own country of mud road and burdock,
filth by the highway   loud and steamy in summer,
low white high school building at the edge of the forest
        her silent friends stand in a straight row—
She was my best good friend—
        they answer the reporters' questions,
country polite   they say   *yes ma'am*   *no sir*

I have filled five books, stacked them
under the window that faces the maple now turning
        red in late September
still I clip and paste, my hands

smudged black with newsprint
       gummy with rubber cement,
              my painless war wounds.

This is the least I can do—
to remember the war in my books.

At the Blue Table

Nothing we do has the quickness, the sureness,
the deep intelligence living at peace would have.
  —Denise Levertov

I went over to your apartment.
We sat at the blue table
talking things over

things that had hurt us
in these days of
too much information.

Someone had forgotten
to tell you something very important
you said & I said

someone yelled at me
for something I forgot to do.
The two of us were drinking tea.

You said *I felt excluded.*
I said *I felt so guilty,*
then you asked

why would they leave me out?
You poured more tea,
a storm was coming, thunder &

lightning at your window.
Well then, we said to each other,
& after that we never spoke again.

Note from My Father

I wake from a dream of wild horses
and remember my father.
Sorrow. Sorrow. Sorrow.
At the end of his life, in the remains
of his literate speech, he was trying
to say something he thought was clever
in garbled nursery rhymes.
He stuttered and stabbed at words.
Like a horse trapped in a forest,
he lifted his head and threw it back,
snorted and cleared his throat.
Then he'd give up and try
to write the thing he wanted me
to know. I think he could smell
his own blood on the places he had
rubbed raw. In my dream the horses
were blue; the trees were red.
In the note, my father said,
you will have   believe me
a crust for a mystic.

Asleep still, I rise

and leave my bed
set out wading the vague air
                                      around my waist
wander from room to room without light
palming the blank spaces   feeling the shadows

 My heavy body falls to the chair
       at my desk, a book opened before me
       a glow off the white pages—
I am reading and writing
                        in the blackened room,
words brilliant and alive
                    my own words
                    not my own words

I stand again and wade
down the stairs, buoyed up,
                       then washed ashore on the orange
couch
soft piles of newsprint on the floor

Singular, predictable   the same rings
of fire and smoke, frequencies
       muffle of chopper blades
       then sharper   red sky, white sand
       choked engines   flash and chemical singe

                sun on green trucks burning oil
                     astringent

Then a sweet breeze from the opened window
inside the safe rooms of the house
                      I have walked and walked asleep
                      all through wakened time
all through the widening water
                          never over my head
in my own body again   unforgotten

Cleaning the Guns

The deer heads were bolted to the wall in my uncles' houses
stuffed & mounted on a plaque. As a child, I was sure
the body of the animal must be behind the wall, as if
it had just poked its antlers through a curtain. Every fall,
two days off from school for the start of deer season
& then dead deer were hung to cool in backyards
from heavy ropes, their eyes still open.
My uncles were all white men who chewed
Mail Pouch tobacco & spit into coffee cans
& all of them were hunters.
I liked to sit on the cement back porch
with my Uncle Ike & help him clean his guns.
We started with his revolver, then the rifles
& last his shotgun—it took all afternoon.
Ike had a white blanket to put the parts on
so they wouldn't get lost & old undershirts I cut up
in little pieces to wrap around the rods. Ike was a machinist
on the railroad & he knew parts. He taught me the names
of each one & it was my job to do the final buff.
After we worked awhile,
he might tell me how he got his deer
this year, or another one from some time back—
the one whose head now hangs over the TV set.
Of course, in a few years he taught me to shoot
& I wasn't bad, but I never went hunting.
Too much trouble I told everyone & by then

I had grown a little scared of him,
but really it was the helplessness
I couldn't get around. The deer absolutely still, alert,
one shot & death. I couldn't do that.
But I did like cleaning the guns,
all the tiny parts—heavier than they looked—
& the requisite precision, the art of it.

Reading Yusef

I'm up early reading
your poems again & picturing
that war, the way I woke
those days on the hard bunk
in my dorm room wondering
who was killed today? who came back?
how broken?—everything I was burning
to know but afraid to hear about.
Once we sat together in
the apartment with the spiral staircase
descending to the dark room of everything,
where you wrote & read & slept—
& yes, there was a saxophone somewhere,
alive with whine & flash & gunfire,
Coltrane above us, or someone
just a little bit like Coltrane,
just a little bit—
& we were facing each other
in the room where we could not turn
around. Your hands were full
of books & papers—mine
were insistently, deliberately
not moving at my sides.
So much I wanted to know
if you could tell me
but I had to leave, something

else to do. It was afternoon
then & me going off into it
to meet that tall white boy who was
plenty mad at me since I was already late
& lost & half asleep with long remembering.
It was as if I could still hear
the dinosaurs crossing the once fertile valley
of the desert snuffling & grunting
like giant javelinas, or the first low
notes of a trombone breaking in
through the oldest silence.
I know how sometimes we
stand between one self & another—
how we can become each other's shadows.
I have listened hard for you,
like trying to follow a whisper
in the wind. Now beneath
the constant rant & roar
I hear you still, when I'm reading
about war, as I was again
this morning, in your poems.

A Drone Poem, Notes For

It's the what-the-hell-is-that? in the sky
      on the highway to Tucson
just the Border Patrol, watching us cross the desert

a *sustained* sound or the *repetition* of one sound:
      Cole Porter's "Night and Day" begins
           with the same note repeated 35 times
      "the monotone of the evening's drone"
      The Velvet Underground's "Heroin"
           binaural alpha tones for deep meditation

The fifth string of the banjo, the dirge string, foam on the upper fret
      mutes the drone
                 & over the left shoulder, hold & thrust
              the drone of the pipes, the breath of the piper

"Nobody watched me before, now I am watched"

Milton: "thrumming the drone of one plaine song"
Lear: "Then kill, kill, kill, kill, kill, kill!"

The boy had a fire engine with lights & remote control,
      Christmas 2001   he made it circle the living room
      Everyone will be rescued   it droned
      No one will be left behind

UAV: unmanned aerial vehicle
snore in the sky, never stops, bees trapped in a Coke bottle
            szvsvzsvzsvszzzzz   mmmmmmmmmm
        the hum ruckles & sneezes, ruckles & weeps
like the growl & sway of the didgeridoo, the beaded eucalyptus limb

Now, not only soldiers go to war
Now, not even soldiers *go to war*

"Pay attention to what they tell you to forget."
The seat of memory in the brain is the seahorse,
        the hippocampus
        train it, train it, train it
"Remembering is repetition anybody can know that"

Learn it by heart
embroider the names in the pith of it,
remember the bees, how they service the queen,
thank them for their service

                        guardian angels of our boots on the ground
                                the angels of death

I have studied the books of war, the mysteries,
the invocations & the desire "to mingle in
        one of those great affairs of the earth"

Silence is one effect of catastrophe
        we hear nothing, no brisance, no roar
we move the way a deer risks a meadow—

we are numb with information, choked by alertness
And death? A breath that goes out & does not return
"Remember the bullet that missed you"

        Have you put ashes on your face and knelt in a ditch?
        Have you worked too hard to understand one thing?
        Have you remembered the names?

"I don't need a weatherman to know which way the wind blows"
the worst things come from the sky
we cannot defend against the sudden, pulled
        down by gravity, building speed—

"Two words—predator drones. You will never see it coming."
        (Barack Obama)

        Have you covered your head in shame?
        Have you remembered what they told us to forget?

The kora of West Africa—twenty-one strings
        makes a thousand names in twine & thread

go little drone
carry the beat of the kora
be hum & yellow
switch & cut, the one bird
holding the circle

"I am nobody; I have nothing to do with explosions."

I was standing "on the pavement, thinking about the government"
        at the corner of Vesey & West Streets watching
                    the burn & the smoke—
"before they came the air had been calm enough."

        I don't want to talk about it
        I can't stand to think about it
        I don't listen to it anymore

Do you think we will now have more women soldiers than men?
All that is needed is a desk, a screen.

Will the men who choose to be "warriors" be more like women?
Will the women and the women-men in the military keep us from war?

We have paid attention.
Have we remembered what they thought we would forget?

                    —*January-June, 2014*

47

Sources and collaborators for this poem include:
Medea Benjamin, Gwendolyn Brooks, the Bureau of Investigative
Journalism, Stephen Crane, Mamadou Diabaté, Bob Dylan,
Philip Glass, Yusef Komunyakaa, Denise Levertov, Hugh Martin,
John Milton, Barack Obama, Bonnie Peterson, Sylvia Plath,
Cole Porter, the Book of Psalms, Adrienne Rich, Muriel Rukeyser,
William Shakespeare, P. W. Singer, Gertrude Stein, Brian Turner,
the Velvet Underground, and Bruce Weigl.

III

"What three things can never be done?
Forget.   Keep silent.   Stand alone."

—Muriel Rukeyser

Our Journey

The palpable is in its place and the impalpable is in its place.
        —Walt Whitman

We drove beside the rivers through the blue smoke & the red sun sharp
        on glass buildings, past the bridges & the windows of the prison
        where dark faces pressed to the light like smudged soot of the old
        city, wisps & leftovers from the mills

You were in your green feathers & your yellow cap, holding my big white
        dog & jug of water, carrying my coins & keys

I was carrying your three valises, the extra tire, the toolbox & the lug wrench

We drove south past the new malls & the red runoff at the strip job &
        we gazed long at the lime-green fields where new lambs rolled
        their heads to get at the swollen teats & nuzzle the warm body
        of their making

The mountains rose like loaves from the wild rivers & we
        followed the Monongahela & the Youghiogheny through the
        gorges to the slow climb up, gears dragging & shifting to
        overtake the semis hauling double-wides on their flatbeds

And came at last to the redbuds just beginning to fill out their colors
            like pursed lips or fresh bruises beside a yellow of forsythia
            thrown over the road cuts on the downgrade

We saw then how quickly the wide sky shifts from bright milk of pale sun
            to ooze of fog & we felt acceleration in our thighs as the rain
            came down heavy on the windshield startling our vision

And we drove to the moon-drenched lake where we listened for the lap
            of the deep water, its riffle in the dark, its pinch & sheen
            & we slept until first light when the geese began their flat
            wet cries, their glides sousing the air with wings

We walked the path we've known all our lives wearing our soft clothes
            & wooden bracelets, so near it was, we could name every weed,
            coltsfoot & trillium, lavender verbena & nests of kingfishers
            in the cottonwood branches lowered to the water the beavers
            dammed up over the winter

You were with me, my most welcome companion, my ambitious bird,
            my left hand, the one who led the damaged children to safety
            in a straight line across the side roads & wet ditches

You have always been with me, in the houses of smoke & oily cinders,
            in back alleys & harbors—you in your purple coat,
            I with my red scarf—in our hard exile & sweet demands

Island

Where are you? Where have you been? How come you here?
  —Poll the parrot, to Robinson Crusoe

Such cities as you could not imagine!
Oh, I could tell you stories!
The waste and darkened places,

corners where the desperate hide,
brick streets of well-kept gardens,
brownstones with heavy walnut doors.

Dust and seed pods on plains that stretch for
centuries across the wide body of a continent,
red with milo, blue with corn.

Landlocked saltwater seas I have waded,
so thick with salt my ankles burned.
Frozen northern lakes where fires

are lit in caves of ice. Underground
it is cool and dark as black marble
and coal dust coats the long wall

and the miners. I know a place where wild
animals are kept behind thick chain link.
I have studied them in my Sunday clothes.

I come from high seas and untrustworthy boats
long becalmed in strange heavy waters.
I came here when things broke down.

I've followed dogs along canals and into meadows
where I gave them their head and they took it.
I trusted them. And now I am with you

on this deserted island where I have given you
a language so you could ask me these questions,
so that I might have a voice to answer to.

Waiting for Jane Austen in Walnut Creek, Ohio, at the end of the twentieth century

If I am a wild Beast I cannot help it.
It is not my own fault.

　　　　—Jane Austen, letter to her sister Cassandra

She was late. Very late, several hundred years to be exact,
and when she finally managed to locate a pay phone and some change
to call, she said she was lost. Something about the SUV
or the landau, outdated maps and a turn north
at the I-77 interchange, which had put her smack
up against Lake Erie just short of the Canadian border.
I gave her new directions. Though I was annoyed, I held my temper.
She got back on the road again, aimed for southern Ohio,

where I was waiting. Waiting for Jane Austen in fog among
the Amish of Ohio with their legendary helpfulness and patience,
their breads and warm pies. On the other side of the fence
behind the motel, two horses at pasture, dark boulders
in gray air. Then I was the one in the eighteenth century,
in the General Store, examining racks of buttons and spools
of thread beside the rakes and ropes as thick as thighs.
Jane was tearing down the highway at 65 m.p.h., a wild Beast
in her worn leather covers and braid of bookmark,
her *apparatus of happiness* fully intact.

Bearded farmers emerged from the mist, spectral in
the rattle, click and wheel of horse and buggy, heard
before seen. I stayed in the shadows, waiting for Jane.

It was early December and unseasonably warm.
The clerk took my money for a small replica
of a leopard stiletto, so camp as to be overly serious,
a symptom of late capitalist iconography, collectible
and valuable. He wrapped my shoe in brown paper.
His overall buttons looked like the whites of your eyes.
From deep in his haystack of whiskers, he announced:
It's too warm for this time of year. Can't tell what
might be coming, strange as this weather has been.

Waiting for Jane on the sidewalk, in the thick of things,
I blended with the black coats and well-behaved children
lining up for the live nativity scene: three wise men
in baggy bathrobes, two shepherds and a woolly sheep,
Joseph and Mary in blue muslin on a pony, all of us singing
"O Come All Ye Faithful." Walnut Creek was all eager delight.
Jane grew later and later and still no one married.
A woman, especially if she have the misfortune of knowing any thing
should conceal it as well as she can. I kept what I knew close to my bosom,
and I had to wait for a very long time. I had told no one of my intentions,
and I had no fortune of my own.

How the Brain Works

Like a peony. Full white blossoms,
heavy and damp with the scurrying
of insects. From this comes language:
Morning sun. Afternoon shower. This, that.
It gathers to fit in open palms, heart shape
that wants to carry one flower as far
as it has to, as fast as it's able, to the dark
oak table, the red cut-glass bowl.
The ants will drop and crawl to the windowsill.
Soft petals will brown and slime,
fall down to re-enter the earth.
And the brain says, *happy.*
The brain says, *do over, do over.*

The Map

Here is the spot where drake and heron
come to feed, the wetlands in Ohio behind
his house. His brilliant mind gave way
beneath an avalanche of random cells
and at the end he slept four days and nights.
I wish I could tell him that this week the tiny
spoons of the dogwood blossoms turned
and drew music up from the drenched ground,
that the redbuds came out all at once,
and trout ran again in the swift streams from the mountains.
One afternoon I read to him *The Old Man and the Sea.*
It was for myself I read, a way to keep company
with him while he was busy with his dying.
It seemed he had found himself in an "unlucky boat."
But when I read the words "big fish," he raised his arm
as if he heard me and recognized, as if he were
about to cast his line out into still water.
By early morning it had begun to rain, or maybe
I dreamed it. Still, I can show you on the map
the place where it happened, right here.

In the Rubble of the World

She finds the arm, or no—
            the *piece* of the arm
                  among small fires and empty hallways
            it's hard to tell the ashes from crushed bone,
she wades dust and paper to find something to use or save—
            pillows or cups, a lamp—
She thinks she sees a piece of fruit under a smoldering sofa
         core and rind   she follows the clues
            for a piece of jewelry   a sleeve
                but it's just this part,
                        this suffix, this—
                            what to do with it?

A strip of inflammable curtain draping
         a desk and chair—swaddling—
this is what comes from searching and saving—
              the relentless percussion of life goes on
        sun and the wicked noises
           march through the air of the brain:
the wounded are never clean—
         like aubergines
                cut open and left to absorb the atmosphere—
          the layered opening of dying roses on a wide table
                  green leaves backlit against the flames
          lint clotted in the heavy drape

Our Lady of the Ruins and Rubble, see
      how the roses shamble and unfurl
      bundle of luster, cluster of light—
         see how the body divides and divides

Signs Following

And these signs shall follow them that believe....
They shall take up serpents; and if they drink
any deadly thing, it shall not hurt them.

      Mark 16: 17-18

When did we think we were safe?
A broom on the porch casts a shadow.
A horse is sliding on snowmelt.
Where are the reins and black saddles?
A truck hauls coal to the railroad, train
of invective, common wailing, wind.
The box of serpents in the brush arbor
rattles, is opened with lifting and shouting,
talking in tongues, redheaded cousin
handles the vipers, circles his
shoulder, wraps the scar on his arm.
How reluctant, the unruly jury, to indict
their neighbor the preacher who led them
out of black hollows, the bright spirit
flashing like high-powered rifle fire,
with signs following dangerous acts.

Too Much, Too Soon Migraine

A study in heterotechnic cooperation:

                                  five guys bent over a carburetor.

Motion sickness

      settles in the middle of my forehead, like a third eye.

Faint hues of ocher or pale egg white,

                              colors we won't speak of in public.

In this large empty space,
a single globe with a chain
makes dust motes shine on the green tile floor
in the spherical shadows,

                        faces show up in digital photographs
                  of empty hallways—state mental hospital
                    closed down in the late 1960s—
power points of light at the empty windows still

jerky ganglia, rigid facial musculature
attention deficit, chaos and mayhem,
just off the radar screen, the coming anarchy.
All my friends do way too much:
work too hard, drive too fast, know
too much, carry too many bags and devices
I run far.   I work out.   Pump

                     iron   *gas*   *up*

Don't blame me for the stuff of change
I too carry

bite off more than I can choose,
                trawl websites on arousal disorders when I can't sleep

Link, link. I am a verb
upload   download
data   data
don't go there

Most of the time
there is nothing coming toward me
                                I'd be pleased to find or sad to lose.

In Real Life

One's real life is often the life that one does not lead.
    —Oscar Wilde

I've been napping in my chair
and have wakened just in time.
Sleeping in the daytime sharpens me
for night life, as if it were my job
to get up and wet down my reeds
to play the clarinet in a small ensemble
where the first set doesn't start till half past ten.
My nap was the color of a moss agate,
gray-green and striped, buffed to sheen
and sweat, the usual nightmares:
the house burns down with all my writing in it;
a famous and successful writer friend offers me her dregs,
Here, take these, I don't need them anymore.
My editor ransacks my closets. His shirt is ripped off
by my faithful and beautiful, half-vicious dog.
In real life, I am planning a new career. I imagine
for myself a small congregation of gay Episcopalians
somewhere in the Midwest, in a town not known for
tolerance, but respectful, even a bit in awe of
anything that passes for style. I am their priest,
their good shepherd, and all my flock play
musical instruments and give amusing dinner parties.
Or, there is the life I seem to have imagined myself into

in which I am cleaning my reeds and shining my shoes
for the band that doesn't exist, in the town I never lived in
playing the instrument I don't know how to play.

The Thing You Can't Forget

It won't let go of your mind,
the over-and-over can't figure it out,
all the secrets, big nuisance, big excuse.
Impatient, unruly, it chokes the imagination
like kudzu sprawled across the roadsides,
overweening "mile-a-minute vine,"
vegetation with no brakes on fecundity,
litter after litter it keeps on.
Kudzu roots make an aromatic jelly,
said to cure a tendency to drink,
and the leaves of the kudzu plant
cover over the useless, the derelict
and abandoned. From this we invent topiary,
fantastic shapes of palaces and creatures,
until the mind can catch what
runs away with it and slow it down,
turning our relentless narratives
into a story we will have to live with.

A Blessing

Inside the mind there is a balm.
I know it and I say hello.
            —Irene McKinney

Translucent braid gelled to silver at first light,
the valley's work, the white, the shining.
An entrenched meander cuts sharp
shoals into the narrow sluice
of the gorge. Clouds like ether rise
from the sandstone up the sheer, simple
mountains, dark-graded with pine.
I come to this water
for the rustle and hiss at the falls,
for the fast train sound when
the traps of the dam open up downriver.
I come for the limestone outcroppings—
the blue stone—and the shift
of the midwinter sandbars after
a summer of drought. I come for
the silence of amber, the flicker
of brook trout over the rapids,
to the soft banks of sand
where the stiff-necked sumac bend
and fall down to what's left
at the end of the river's dry branch.

In the Sidney Lanier Best Western Motel in Gainesville, Georgia, I think of the great Polish poet

Wisława Szymborska, who wrote that she
"believes in the wasted years of work."
I read this on the airplane yesterday.
What did she mean by "waste?"
What did she mean by "work?"
This town is "the poultry capital of the world."
Was it in Georgia or North Carolina
where all the workers died in a chicken factory fire
because the owners had locked the doors
from the outside against the union organizers?

Last night at dinner, we wondered,
How long does it take to write a poem?
On the average. Considering
I have written some poems in twenty minutes
and some poems I've been writing for twenty years,
I guess the average would be about two to five years.
And of course the rest of my life, which is
half a century, plus a few years.

But we'd have to subtract the time required
for raising children, and for the long distractions of grief:
a year or two for grandparents, and for parents maybe
six to eight years depending on how many you had to begin with—
and that's not counting friends, ex-lovers, or beloved pets.

And at least five years for partners and for the loss
of a child the years are uncountable, years with no heart
and no thought. And if one allows for the toll anyone's job
can take in time, human tiredness, real or imagined
reprisals, the slow dull days without thinking
one single original thought, well then one poem
could take a whole lifetime, and much of any lifetime
is waste, isn't it? For example,

I could be doing any number of things this morning
besides writing here, but since the great expatriate
Henry James wrote: "A writer is one on whom nothing
is wasted," I am sitting in a mauve and green room
in Georgia, in a motel named for a poet, writing down
what I am thinking at the moment. I am letting this
place have its way with me, as James Wright did
lying in his hammock trying to find language
for what appeared to him: "the bronze butterfly,"
"the distances of the late afternoon." At the end of his poem
he famously wrote, "I have wasted my life."

I prefer Szymborska. Whatever wasted years are
she believes in them. That they are taking us somewhere
we need to go, like the winning football team, "The Poets,"
in another state where the southern poet Andrew Hudgins

graduated from Sidney Lanier High School.
Can anyone call to mind a line or two from Sidney Lanier?
And if not, were all his years of work "wasted?"

We do not like to say so. And this is not
where I wanted my poem to end up.
On the Main Street of Gainesville, Georgia,
is a bronze chicken. Today I will read
some of my poems to the students
of Brenau University. This is my work.
And I believe in it: the waste,
the distances of the mornings,
the ice bucket, and the armoire with the TV set inside.

And then I arrive at the powerful green hill

Up, up, I follow
          the creek bed through downed branches
                    on spongy leaves, rimed and slippery.
The way is clear because
it is late winter,
          wet snow patches
                    the runoff cold, cold to the touch
                    a tang of ice still in it.

And then I arrive at the powerful green hill,
my place, my exact location,
          where I began and started from
                    where I will end beneath this ground.
I have brought everything I've left undone—
letters and resolutions, almost loves,
          hard grudges—to give to the wind that takes them up,
                    tosses them down, down until
my hands are empty and I am as thin and light as a girl.

Notes

The epigraphs to the sections are from: Elizabeth Bishop, "Crusoe in England"; Charles Wright, "A Short History of My Life"; and Muriel Rukeyser, "The Book of the Dead."

"Biography" takes its first line and its form from Henri Cole's poem, "Self-Portrait in a Gold Kimono."

"The Greeks of 1983": The epigraph from Cavafy is from his poem, "Ithaka," as translated by Edmund Keeley and Philip Sherrard.

"The Wave": The epigraph is from Osip Mandelstam's poem, "Tristia," as translated by Clarence Brown and W.S. Merwin.

"Ars Poetica": The epigraph is from the poem, "Knife," by Charles Simic.

"Beautiful War" refers to events and photographs from the first six months following the U.S. invasion of Iraq in March 2003. PFC Jessica Lynch from Palestine, West Virginia, was serving in Iraq when she was injured in a vehicular accident and then taken by Iraqi forces. In April 2003 she was brought home as a hero, the first successful rescue of an American POW since World War II and the first rescue of a woman. The story of Private Lynch fighting off Iraqi soldiers and escaping to be dramatically rescued made good media copy but turned out to have been utterly fabricated. Lynch told the true story—that she never fired her weapon and that she was competently cared for in a military hospital—to the media and in 2007 to the U.S. Congress. In her testimony she blamed the media and the military for deliberately lying for their own gain. "They should have found out the facts before they spread the word like wildfire," she said.

"At the Blue Table": The epigraph is from Denise Levertov's poem, "Life at War."

"A Drone Poem, Notes For": This poem was created in collaboration with fabric artist Bonnie Peterson as a part of the 2014 "Poetic Dialogue" project curated by artist Beth Shadur and exhibited at the Ukrainian Institute of Modern Art in Chicago in 2015.

"Our Journey" is dedicated to Lynn Emanuel, most welcome companion.

"Waiting for Jane Austen in Walnut Grove, Ohio, at the end of the twentieth century": The quoted lines in the poem are from Jane Austen's *Northanger Abbey* (1818). The poem is dedicated to Judith Vollmer.

"The Map" is in memory of Stephen P. Witte (1943-2004).

"In the Rubble of the World" includes several lines from Eleanor Wilner's poem, "Trümmerfrauen (The Rubble-Women)."

"A Blessing": The epigraph is from Irene McKinney's poem, "Bravery." The poem is dedicated to her, *in memoriam*.

"In the Sidney Lanier Best Western Motel in Gainesville, Georgia I think of the great Polish poet": Sidney Lanier (1842-1881), born in Macon, Georgia, was a writer and musician noted for his melodic poems, including "The Marshes of Glynn" (1878). Lake Lanier in central Georgia is named for him, as is the Sidney Lanier Bridge in Brunswick, Georgia, and at least one Best Western Motel. Many thanks to friends on the Georgia Poetry Circuit (2001-02) whose kindness, wit, and generosity helped to make this poem.

"And then I arrive at the powerful green hill": The title and the italicized line in this poem are from Muriel Rukeyser's poem "Then I Saw What the Calling Was."

Acknowledgments

I gratefully acknowledge the editors and staff of the journals in which some of the poems in this book first appeared, sometimes in different versions or under different titles:

Alaska Quarterly Review, The American Voice, Artful Dodge, Bloom, Court Green, Crab Orchard Review, The Georgia Review, Great River Review, The Iron Mountain Review, The Kenyon Review Online, New Letters, Pleiades, Prairie Schooner, Shenandoah, and *Third Coast.*

"The Sleep Writer" and "At the Border" were originally published in *Windfall: New and Selected Poems* by Maggie Anderson (University of Pittsburgh Press, 2000).

"Black Overcoat" received the Glenna Luschei Award from *Prairie Schooner* 2008.

"A Drone Poem, Notes For" was created as a collaborative work with fabric artist Bonnie Peterson for the "Poetic Dialogue" project curated by Beth Shadur and exhibited at the Ukrainian Institute of Modern Art in Chicago in 2015. The poem is also included in the anthology, *Poems and Their Making: A Conversation,* edited by Philip Brady (Etruscan Press, 2015).

"*And then I arrive at the powerful green hill,*" "How the Brain Works," and "Beautiful War" were also published in *The Autumn House Anthology of Contemporary American Poetry,* edited by Michael Simms. (Autumn House Press, 2nd and 3rd Editions, 2011, 2015).

"How the Brain Works" was also published in *Translators Writing, Writing Translators,* edited by Françoise Massardier-Kenney, et.al. (The Kent State University Press, 2016).

"*And then I arrive at the powerful green hill*" and "A Blessing" were also published in *Eyes Glowing at the Edge of the Woods: Fiction and Poetry from West Virginia,* edited by Laura Long and Doug Van Gundy (West Virginia University Press, 2017).

I am grateful to the following for essential gifts of money, time, and a place to work: the Research Council, the Department of English, and the Wick Poetry Center at Kent State University; the National Endowment for the Arts; the Ohio Arts Council; the MacDowell Colony; the Anderson Center for Interdisciplinary Studies; the Virginia Center for the Creative Arts; and the Aalborg University Center *Institut for Sprog og Kultur* in Aalborg, Denmark. I offer heartfelt gratitude and love to Robert and Walter Wick and their families for their generosity and vision in creating the Wick Poetry Center at Kent State University in memory of their sons, Stan and Tom.

It has been my good fortune to have many writers, colleagues, and friends who have read, reread, and commented on these poems in various versions over years. I thank them *all* for their patience, attention and care. I give my most enthusiastic thanks to the wonderful staff at Four Way Books: Sally Ball, Clarissa Long, Ryan Murphy—and the incomparable Martha Rhodes.

Finally, to these dear ones, I give deepest thanks for their consistent inspiration and sustenance both to me and to my work from earliest beginnings to the present—*ne plus ultra*: Jan Beatty, Lynn Emanuel, Anna French, Winston Fuller, Judith Kirman, Carol Maier, Ed Ochester, Maxine Scates, Judith Gold Stitzel, Jean Valentine, Judith Vollmer—and *in memoriam*: Gwendolyn Brooks, Patricia Dobler, William Matthews, Irene McKinney, and Louise McNeill.

Maggie Anderson is the author of four previous books of poetry: *Windfall: New and Selected Poems*, *A Space Filled with Moving*, *Cold Comfort*, and *Years That Answer*. She has co-edited several thematic anthologies, including *A Gathering of Poets*, a collection of poems read at the 20th anniversary commemoration of the shootings at Kent State University in 1970, as well as *Learning by Heart: Contemporary American Poetry about School* and *After the Bell: Contemporary American Prose about School*. Her awards include two fellowships from the National Endowment for the Arts, fellowships from the Ohio, Pennsylvania, and West Virginia councils on the arts, and the Ohioana Library Award for contributions to the literary arts in Ohio. The founding director of the Wick Poetry Center and of the Wick Poetry Series of the Kent State University Press, Anderson is professor emerita of English at Kent State University and now lives in Asheville, North Carolina.